Read Here First!

This book is 2 in 1, *"*From The Hood*"* and *"*How To Not Sound Like An Ignorant Bozo*."*

As many of you know, I prefer to be informal and write in an everyday tone. Sophisticated language and presentation tend to leave out a lot of people and I want to be inclusive. If you come across words you're not completely familiar with, I encourage you to look them up. Some people have a tendency to ignore the word they don't know, but that can prevent you from grasping the whole point. Yes, one word can make a big difference. I learned that lesson in college the hard way. Also, how can you expand your vocabulary and knowledge if you just skip the unknown instead of learning it?

I can't express how crucial emotional intelligence is to understanding my books and life in general. Emotional intelligence is emotional control and the ability to recognize, process, and be mindful of your emotions and those of other people. No matter your gender, age, or race, you are a being who functions on emotions. They fuel our decisions and reactions even when we think they don't. Emotional intelligence will allow you to receive what is being presented, even when it's the unfavorable truth.

The following topics can be controversial and I'm aware of how people often react. Most of the time people are either offended by my direct presentation, they're unwilling to accept the truth, or they confuse the point being made with their incorrect assumptions. If you get offended by what you read, try to find exactly why you feel that way. Our emotions or ego can make it hard to see things for what they are and defensiveness can get the best of us. To help avoid that, I recommend frequently questioning the 'why.' For example, why do I feel this way, why would someone say that, or why is this my perception. I also recommend being as critical of yourself as you would a stranger. For example, ask yourself if you would accept a stranger having your same explanation or behavior.

If you notice yourself getting defensive, pause and remember why you're reading this book and why I wrote it. I want people to be their best. The topics I write about are ones which heavily affect our society, more so because people don't know how to process them. If people aren't processing, we're not evolving. Although I am direct, my purpose isn't to be malicious. My purpose is to shine light on the emotions and issues people aren't processing. Life is direct, not sugar coated. I am simply acknowledging the directness we're all already surrounded by.

**Enjoy,
pass it on, &
post on social media!**

From The Hood:
Don't Be The Useless Idiot They Assume You Are

Yes, I'm from the hood, the block, city of chiques, or however you refer to it. I love the hood! I can pay bills, go shopping, and buy food all in one laundromat. Who needs Postmates when there is the all inclusive ice cream truck, homeboy driving by with pizzas, la señora with tamales, and the elotero (corn man)? As much as I love the hood, it's hard to ignore how much we tend to play in to the idiot role people assume of us. Let's be real and go down the list of how people view us. They think we're slobs, lazy, stupid, uneducated, and a waste of life. Yes, even if you spent all your money on that nice ride and try to flaunt like you don't share a room with five other people. If you live in the hood, no amount of flashiness is louder than where you can afford to live.

Sh!t Adds Up!

Are we slobs, lazy, stupid, uneducated, and a waste of life? If I was an outsider judging from what I can see, I would say yes. How could someone conclude any different when there is trash everywhere, things always being broken, many people refuse to learn new things, parents let their kids do whatever they please, and many people refuse to engage in activities to make their surroundings better. I know some people will disagree with that description so let me ask you a couple questions. When you envision wealthier neighborhoods, how would you describe them and their people? How are the hood and wealthier neighborhoods the same and different? It's easier for people to see the negative truth about something they're tied to when it's directly compared to its opposite.

Obviously wealthier neighborhoods have more money in them, but does that really explain the negatives I mentioned? Does it explain the dirtiness? No. If I asked people individually if they're a slob or lazy, most would probably say no. So how does that add up to the hood looking dirty? Do you ever litter, leave trash somewhere other than a trash can? Do you leave your animal's poop in public? Do you ignore the trash and poop left by others? Have you specifically taught your kids not to litter? If you know your answer is yes to any of the first three questions or no to the last one, you are a contributor. Rather than trying to explain why you're not a contributor or pointing out what other people do wrong, let's take a mature and productive approach.

Understand, if you're from the hood, it represents you whether you want it to or not. When people see or hear where you come from, the characteristics of the hood are stuck on you like a tire boot. That's one reason to be a part of the solution. Which brings me to a major difference between people from the hood and people from wealthier neighborhoods. People from wealthier neighborhoods tend to take ownership of their surroundings. They understand their space doesn't end at their doorstep. Although the community doesn't exclusively belong to them, their money contributes to it. Beyond the money, the community is where they spend their time, raise kids, and live. Just like in their personal living quarters, they smell the smells, walk among the conditions, and are affected by the surroundings. All those things are true for us in the hood too, including our money contributing. The difference is, people in the hood don't tend to take ownership.

We see trash and act like it's not our problem. That's a flawed mentality. You may not do the littering, but if you have to live among it and people see it as a representation of you, it's your problem. If your kids are the ones littering, it's your problem. If you pay taxes from your wages, your shopping, your car registration, or any other form, it's your problem. The government does slack on doing their part, but doesn't it seem weird to expect the government to care about us more than we care about ourselves and each other? If we aren't willing to take a few seconds to throw our own trash away or pick up someone else's, why be upset at the government for slacking just like us?

Don't get me wrong, I agree the government needs to do better, but that doesn't make it any less true that we all need to do better. Both are true. It doesn't make sense to wait until the government steps up before we do anything, when we are the ones who deal with the repercussions. That makes as much sense as refusing to do anything to help the leak in your roof until maintenance comes to fix it. Aren't you, your family, and belongings the ones suffering the consequences?

What you've read so far is hard for many people to accept. If it's hard for you or you deny you're part of the problem, that's telling you something. It means you recognize what the problematic behavior is and you don't want to be associated with it. That's good! Now we need to turn that recognition in to a solution that actually works. Our tendencies of denying and avoidance don't actually do what we think they do. They do the opposite. In order to actually not be a part of the problem, you need to actively be a part of the solution, not passive.

As someone who has personally gone through the change, it honestly isn't hard or the hassle I thought it would be. For example, when I pick up my dog's poop, I pick up any surrounding poop until the bag I have is full. It literally takes a few seconds and I already have the bag in my hand anyway. Of course it would be nice if more people took responsibility and picked up their own poop to begin with, but until that happens, I still want to enjoy not stepping in it or smelling it. If you've ever seen how poop can add up, even from tiny dogs, you can understand a basic concept many people tend to overlook. Sh!t adds up! Remember this when you feel like your small act of picking something up won't matter. If it added up one small poop at a time, one small act will add up just the same.

Individually, we have the tendency to think what we do doesn't matter because we're a small contribution. Look at all the trash you see in the streets. It isn't from someone dumping a huge load. It's from one person who thought their "small" litter wouldn't be a big deal, multiplied by millions of other people who also thought the same thing. The trash you see is one parent failing to teach their kid about littering, multiplied by millions of other untaught kids. When we are self absorbed or narrow minded, we miss the reality. The neglect you see in the hood is from one person not caring, multiplied by a million others not caring. All we need to do is switch it. It begins with your actions. Just do your small part and let it add up.

Stupid & Uneducated

Growing up, I thought I was stupid and incapable of learning. Of course it didn't help my parent called me stupid, but in adulthood I realized it's a common insecurity in people from the hood. When you're surrounded by broken things, trash, and non hood teachers reminding you that you'll never make it beyond your current environment, it makes sense to think that way. Through a miracle I made it to college 2 days before the semester began. It was in a White city, seven hours away in Chico, California. The culture shock hit me like a cold glass of ice.

Being surrounded by White people and scholars increased my feelings of stupidity, but the feedback my professor gave me on my first college paper was a breaking point. In a nice, but direct way, she basically told me I was far below my age range and was unsure how I even made it to college. I was too far from home to go back and I wasn't about to tell my parent I was just as stupid as they said I was. I began studying seven days a week, day and night, sought extra tutoring resources, sat in the front of my classes, *SOUGHT CONSTRUCTIVE CRITICISM OF MY ABILITIES*, spoke frequently to professors, and took every opportunity to learn anything. Long story short, I graduated in four years at the top of my class and went on to complete my master's degree in a class full of career professionals two and three times my age.

Seeking constructive criticism instead of relying on only your self evaluations ensures you're doing your best. If you cannot handle feedback, you're likely not operating at the maturity level you assume you are. Self-awareness and emotional intelligence are good topics to explore for improvement.

As it turns out, I'm not stupid! I was a product of my sh!t home, sh!t school, and sh!t community environment. Imagine that. A person going their whole life blinded and misguided by their circumstances. Some of you have been living a false life feeling stuck, stupid, or incapable simply because you're unaware. You can do and be better, but you have to do things different. Especially if your parents passed down their feelings of helplessness and stupidity to you. Although I recommend college (not online) because the diverse atmosphere multiplies the book knowledge you gain, it's

NOT the only way for you to become educated. You can actively seek knowledge through reading, watching, and listening.

How To Be Better

If you only have a high school education or lower, you refuse to read, AND you don't really engage in information seeking activities, you will likely be as stupid as people think you are. It's not your fault you were given sh!t circumstances, but now that you've read this, it's on you to make the choice to better yourself. If the description at the beginning of this paragraph describes you and you're reading this thinking you're fine, you're blind. Most likely you're just too naïve to grasp how closed your mind is and how little you know. If the description at the beginning describes you and you think there is no hope for you because you're just stupid, you're blind. Unless you make a deliberate effort to do things different from what you normally do, how do you know you're just stupid?

There is a whole world of psychology and research about you and the hood that you're completely unaware of. There are numerous studies about poor people, race, gender, and just about any of your characteristics you can think of. Explore them and you'll likely see you're just like millions of other people in harsh surroundings. If you can recognize how people from privileged surroundings tend to be products of their environment, you can recognize how you might be a product as well. If you understand this concept and you can accept constructive criticism, you can be better. The only thing that makes you stupid, is willfully choosing to remain ignorant.

You have to recognize your environment for what it is. We tend to have backward thinking in the hood. A lot of what we know is incorrect and literally the opposite of reality. For example, many of us think politics don't have anything to do with us. The truth is, EVERYTHING in your life involves politics, you just don't know any better. Your nearby food options, quality of schools, your job, clothes, any assistance programs, prices you pay, free services, nearby noisy factories, internet availability, pothole streets, and any random thing you can think of. Even the commercials shown in your area. Politics affect everybody, rich and poor, but the poor are the ones who get screwed over. Our refusal to get involved and be informed is a huge reason for that. I'm not saying to become a politician, but why would you not want to be informed about what directly affects you?

Many of us feel like we don't have any power anyways so f*ck it. It's not that we don't have power, but we, who are not rich, have to rely on each other to have a strong voice and collective money power. How can we rely on each other when many of us choose to not get involved? The irony is, rich people rely on our collective money too and their power comes from us remaining ignorant and separate. Think about it. How is Walmart a multibillion dollar company? Just so you know, with just one billion dollars you can afford to spend $5,000 every day for over 500 years. Anyway, their money comes from us shopping there. The work force they depend on to collect that money comes from us too. Without shoppers or even with shoppers, but no employees to work, can they still make money? No.

Basic math, where would Walmart be if we did our part and put our collective money power together for our own good? They'd either be out of business or giving their employees better money and benefits. It really is that simple. The hard part is getting people to learn how simple it is and how to stop being too scared to make a scene. It'll take time for you to learn politics, but meanwhile here is a tip to follow. When poor people, people of color, lgbtq+, the disabled, environmentalist, and any historically disenfranchised group boycott something, you do the same. No matter your views of lgbtq+ or even if you're not poor, every group I named has the same threat to their income and wellbeing.

UPDATE: For those who were skeptical of my talk of power, the COVID-19 disaster just gave you a fine example. Immediately there was a chain reaction of financial struggle, including for big businesses and oil companies. It's real simple, people stayed home and businesses began losing money. Suddenly the lowest level of workers became essential, when previously many people thought of them as unimportant. The reality is they were always essential, many people just don't have the thought process to realize it until something is missing.

A lot of people think this stuff is silly or pointless, but ask yourself some questions. What's your highest education level? Realistically, does your education level or reading habit provide you with a sufficient amount of knowledge to make an informed decision? Are you comfortable living up to the negative stereotypes people expect of you? If not, how do you expect to be different if you keep doing exactly what you've always done and aren't willing to try change? If you're not a heterosexual White man, the ONLY reason why you can generally go about your life freely today, is because people were willing to do the things people often call silly or pointless.

Once you start to get informed, the world and your situation will start to look a lot different. You cannot change or do anything different without getting informed. It's the foundation for everything. Again, you don't have to go to formal college or become a politician. You're literally surrounded by information with tv, the internet, the library, and free local resources. Take advantage of them. If you don't read well, try kids books, audiobooks, and listening to National Public Radio (NPR- npr.org). It doesn't matter what topic you start with as long as you let it guide you to others. This means ask questions about what you read, seek the answers to them, and explore ideas you're unfamiliar with. If you're stuck, some good starting topics are: emotional intelligence, anything under psychology or sociology, parenting, and the civil rights they don't teach in high school.

Where You Are

I'll be honest, I hate history. The old dates sound foreign and it's always the same story of immoral White men desperately trying to prevent any non White from showing them up. However, as an adult seeking information, I found out there is a whole hidden history that is interesting and fills in a lot of gaps. Did you know hoods were actually created by White people not too long ago? They deliberately made separate neighborhoods for people of color and marked them as bad simply because they were not White. They deliberately minimized the resources to them while maximizing resources to Whites, deliberately prevented development from thriving, and made it a point to reserve loans mainly for Whites. Don't take my word for it, look up *neighborhood redlining*. There is a reason you are where you are and up until now, your family line was unaware things could be different. You're likely the first one to see the reality. Don't continue the stereotypical cycle.

Many people tend to retell history in terms of only Black and White people. Racist policies and discrimination affected ALL people of color. If a source only mentions Black people, they're likely misspeaking or omitting other people of color.

~End Of Book 1~

How To Not Sound Like An Ignorant Bozo:
A Guide To Having Educated Opinions

It's cool we can all have our opinions, buuut it's getting a bit ridiculous. As we advance in science and our ability to have unlimited access to knowledge, the more absurd it is to have such stupid and baseless opinions! Most people pride themself in knowing things and don't want to sound like an ignorant bozo. So how can people be so comfortable having opinions that are based on nothing more than their own opinions? Despite our confidence in our ability to form opinions, it's not exactly the most logical way to present ourself as an informed individual.

For all you die hard, 'I'm entitled to my own opinion, it's my right' folks, no one is trying to prevent you from having an opinion. I want you to have the best opinions! To be clear, this book isn't referring to the insignificant opinions which only affect you, such as a color preference. It's referring to opinions which tend to guide how you work, treat others, raise kids, vote, and other actions which directly affect your loved ones and strangers around you. You should want to have educated opinions so you won't be an ignorant bozo.

I want us all to have educated opinions because we all exist in the same world and depend on each other throughout our day to day lives. You may feel like you personally don't have an affect on people, but think of how many days a week you interact with people at any given moment. Think about ordering food, driving, working, utilizing public facilities, living among neighbors, etc. The reality is, no matter how much we think we don't, we affect each other. It seems more productive for everyone to work on being their best self, rather than just point a finger at someone else to be better while we do nothing. If everyone just relies on their pointing finger, what change is actually happening? Not much!

UPDATE: The COVID-19 disaster is also a perfect example of how every. single. one of us affects each other. People caught the virus from unknown strangers minding their own business, everyone had to obey some type of order no matter their circumstances, people stayed home and decreased the opportunities of criminals, people got to work much faster because of no traffic, and residential trash workers became overwhelmed by people staying home and producing more waste, while industrial trash workers saw a decrease in work. Any random job or person you can think of was affected in some way.

The following are quick ways to determine if it's time to rethink your opinion. For some people, quick ways to determine if your "facts" are really opinions that should be rethought.

-If it generally aligns with your parents way of thinking, especially if they're uneducated. The reality is, humans were not as informed years ago as we are today. Not too long ago people were panicked and thought the world was ending in Y2K! Yes, people were literally rushing to buy all the water, food, and sand bags like it was some type of storm.

-If it involves a topic you don't have personal experience with or an education in. Let's be real, it's not exactly logical to make an assumption on something you haven't had the opportunity to acquire knowledge about. It's a major flaw of the human condition.

-If it's generally the same thing you believed as a minor or young adult.

-If it involves a topic you've never actually researched.
-If it comes from your religious institution. As much as we love our religions, the fact is, religions often go directly against what science shows to be true. Don't act like you don't believe in science because it's the reason you can read this and the reason you can travel safely throughout traffic light controlled streets. Everything you do involves science. Even eating.

-If it's a popular opinion. Popular and logic don't often exist together.

-If it involves you questioning research, but you don't have a college education and you haven't actually read the related studies. All things should be questioned by people at all levels, but people should also understand their own limitations. College is where people gain a deeper understanding of research and how to conduct it. Unless you self educate, most people without a college education are naturally going to be limited in their understanding of research. Studies usually address various questions and concerns in detail, which can help people with a limited understanding, but most people don't actually read them.

How To Correct Yourself

There are two major components to forming educated opinions. The obvious is acquiring knowledge (any information). The more information you gather from experiences, informational resources, nature, and anywhere in life, the more equipped you are. Information is literally everywhere and in everything. However, if we just rely on the information we receive in our day to day activities, our intake will typically be limited. Think about your normal day. Going to work, maybe some other place, and then home or whatever your routine. How much and how often do you learn anything in your normal day?

If reading more and school aren't real options for you to explore, consider the following ways of obtaining more knowledge. Listen to NPR (National Public Radio) instead of your normal music station, watch informative tv such as National Geographic or History Channel, converse with people you probably wouldn't have anything in common with, analyze how/why you're different and similar to your parents or guardians, sit and watch bugs/animals and question their behavior, or do an activity different from what you would normally choose. Such activities may not sound like much, but we tend to take the everyday things we know and see for granted. If that sounds silly or cliche, go to a place you've never been, where you have a language barrier. You'll understand immediately.

The second MAJOR component of forming educated opinions is emotional intelligence, which comes from <u>DEVELOPING</u> self-awareness. Developing is emphasized because self-awareness and emotional intelligence are not automatically acquired, as many people wrongly assume. They require effort and thought. The name emotional intelligence might make you think, 'wtf do emotions have to do with this book.' The answer is EVERYTHING. Everything we do and don't do is guided by emotions either directly or indirectly. You might eat sweets because they make you feel happy, maybe you go to work for fear of not having money, maybe you helped someone to prove your love, or maybe you went on a crime spree because you were angry with your life. Emotional intelligence, which is not as common as people like to think, is what allows us to be well rounded individuals who can appropriately process life and react to situations.

Humans, no matter how smart or educated, cannot be all knowing. There will always be times where we're wrong or blinded, **no matter who we are.** The difference between being a bozo and being mistaken or having a lapse in judgement, is having the emotional intelligence to recognize your shortcomings and admitting when you're wrong. People with emotional intelligence understand they're capable of being wrong, even when they're well informed and have the sense to recheck their facts when they're met with opposing information. They also understand something isn't necessarily true just because they've always believed it to be and understand their experiences are not the only ones that exist. Emotionally intelligent people don't live life refuting new information just because it's uncomfortable to receive or different from what they've always known. Modern medicine, cars, and phones were once new and shocking, now look at us. Let's not let 'new' intimidate us! Let's allow it to help us be the well informed people we assume we are.

Real Life Example

Let's quickly examine a controversial topic which requires a high degree of emotional intelligence, racism. This requires a great deal of emotional intelligence no matter what role you think it does or doesn't play in your life. There are people who think it isn't an issue anymore, people who think it is every issue, and people who think it's appropriate. All three are uneducated opinions to have. First, racism is still a prevalent issue and there are decades worth of data to show it. Self-aware people with emotional intelligence who are unfamiliar with racism and the existing data understand they have much to learn. They know their own lack of experience with it doesn't determine its existence and understand they're not in a position to refute the knowledge and experiences of informed people. As uncomfortable as the topic is, they understand their discomfort is minimal in comparison to the discomfort and damage racism causes. Emotionally intelligent people understand it must be dealt with in order to be fixed and, like any issue in life, ignoring it doesn't actually make it go away.

Self-aware people with emotional intelligence who are informed about racism understand despite its prevalence, it's not the basis for all issues. Assuming it's a non issue and assuming it's every issue, are both extreme opinions on different ends of the spectrum. Both are problematic and lack the emotional intelligence needed for balance. An inability to balance means an inability to process the associated facts for what they are. Which leads us to the emotionally intelligent person who views racism as appropriate. Just kidding, an emotionally intelligent person with such views doesn't exist. Despite the hate and superiority often involved, racism literally boils down to extreme stupidity. You will never find a racist who relies on actual facts, isn't living a life of hypocrisy and contradiction, or has the appropriate level of self-awareness needed for emotional intelligence. If they had self-awareness, they wouldn't be a racist because they would have the ability to decipher reality from their misinterpretations of life.

Important!

On your journey to forming educated opinions, get out of the habit of 'all or nothing' thinking. This common pitfall prevents people from being thorough and well rounded thinkers. Just about everything has pros and cons and can be good or bad depending on the circumstances and objectives. Let's use science as an example. There are people who refute science because 'it isn't accurate.' Although science is flawed (like everything else in life), to simply write it off as inaccurate is illogical. Science saves lives, allows us to be advanced civilizations, allows us to solve crimes, and gives us answers that would otherwise go unknown. The smarter way to treat science is to accept it, but also be mindful of ways it can fall short. Ask questions, weigh the pros and cons, and compare findings to other areas of life. Be analytical, not all or nothing.

Conclusion

Below are random topics the average person has misinformed opinions about. I encourage you to explore them, even if you assume your opinion is common sense. The following all have a ton of research on them and will be easy to find. Don't stop here. Take any random opinion you have and explore it. Be mindful, there are sources to support every opinion, even the factually incorrect ones. Try to stick with official (i.e government sources) and scholarly sources. NPR (National Public Radio) is a well rounded organization with a wide variety of shows that will get you on the right track. You can find your local station on their website listed at the end of this book.

- Crime trends and who commits what. The average person has misperceptions about race, ignores the gender difference, and incorrectly perceives crime to be on a steady increase. People also have a tendency to focus their concerns on popular misperceptions, rather than actual trends. Did you know, in most violent crimes the victim and offender are of the same race?

- Homeless populations and costs. The average person is misinformed about who the homeless are and what are cost effective and productive ways of handling their issue. Did you know there are years of research which show it's cheaper and more productive to help them with their basic needs?

- Intelligence and self-awareness. Many of you might have an OMG moment when you check out how people tend to perceive their own intelligence and capabilities. It's quite alarming. If it doesn't come up in your searches, google the 'Dunning-Kruger Effect'.

- Sex education. Most people don't actually have thorough and accurate knowledge. Most states don't require comprehensive and accurate sex ed. and it shows in our health and pregnancy statistics. States who adhere to a religious model rather than a scientifically accurate one, tend to be worse off. Sex education isn't sinful, it's a matter of public health and wellbeing.

- Race and ethnicity. This should be an easy topic to be informed about because our entire history is based on it and it's literally everywhere we look. Unfortunately, too many people are unaware of all the up to date research and statistics that can clear up popular misconceptions. Pick a racial fact you assume to be true and google it. You can also check out my short book *White People Expectations You Have.*

- Politics and who is affected by it. It's a common position for people to think politics has nothing to do with them, but there is not one activity you can engage in that doesn't involve it. I thought I wasn't interested in politics, but after I became educated I realized I was just put off by the language because I couldn't understand it. It's amazing how my brain automatically tuned out what I couldn't understand. One day I all of a sudden heard what was being said on the news. Maybe you're not uninterested, they're just speaking a language you don't know. Learn it in your own way.

- Differences between males and females. Most of us feel like experts in this department because we've encountered males and females our whole lives. See if your knowledge actually holds up against research and statistics! If you believe the popular idea women are emotional and men aren't, you're in for a surprise. Here are two hints, anger is an emotion and believing only women are emotional requires ignoring all the glaring statistics on violence.

Other Easy Reads By The G.:

"White People Expectations You Have:
A Basic Sense Approach To Racism"

"YOU Will Succeed With This Guide:
For ALL College Bound People.
Even Those Who Struggle"

Random Helpful & Reliable Sources:

NPR.org- National Public Radio. News, true stories, investigative journalism, politics, brain games, and more.

APA.org- American Psychological Association. Research, help center resources, educational networks, and more.

FBI.gov- Federal Bureau of Investigation. Crime data and statistics, safety information, tips, and more.

asanet.org- American Sociological Association. Research, educational information, educator resources, journals, and more.

justice.gov- Department of Justice. Statistics, information, victim resources, and more.

scholar.google.com- A search engine to find scholarly sources.